Rusty The Elevator Dog

by Nancy Salerno

RUSTY THE ELEVATOR DOG

Copyright © 2016 by Nancy Salerno

ISBN-13: 978-0-69273384-4
ISBN-10: 0-692-73384-1

Library of Congress PCN: 2016943927

All Rights Reserved. No parts of this book may be reproduced or utilized in any form or by any means, electronic or mechanical, including photocopying, scanning, recording, or by any information storage and retrieval system known or hereafter invented, without permission, in writing from the publisher.

To obtain a copy of this book,
please visit www.amitypublications.com

Published by
AMITY Publications
Barrington, NH 03825

Printed in the United States of America

Dedicated to . . .

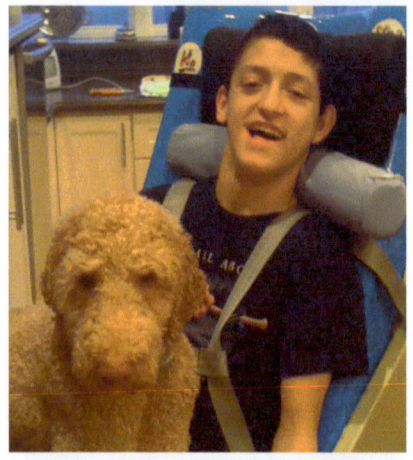

My son, Nicholas, who inspires me every day.

And . . .

Our beloved,
fun loving
Goldendoodle,
Rusty.

Rusty is a Goldendoodle. He is a big dog with lots of curly hair. Rusty is the color of apricots with one white patch of hair on his chest.

Rusty came to our family from Manitoba, Canada, on a big jet plane. The plane was loud and noisy.

Rusty is afraid to fly.

When Rusty met our family for the first time,

he did not want to come out of his crate.

He was shivering and shaking.

Rusty is afraid of meeting new people.

Rusty does not like to play outside because of loud noises like airplanes flying overhead, trucks going by, and other dogs barking.

Rusty is afraid to play outside.

Rusty is especially afraid of thunderstorms.

He runs and hides in the shower.

His teeth chatter and he shakes with fear.

However, there is one noise that does not frighten him. Rusty is not afraid of the sound of our elevator.

He loves to go in the elevator with Nick.

Nick has a disability called Cerebral Palsy.

He uses a wheelchair to get around because he cannot walk.

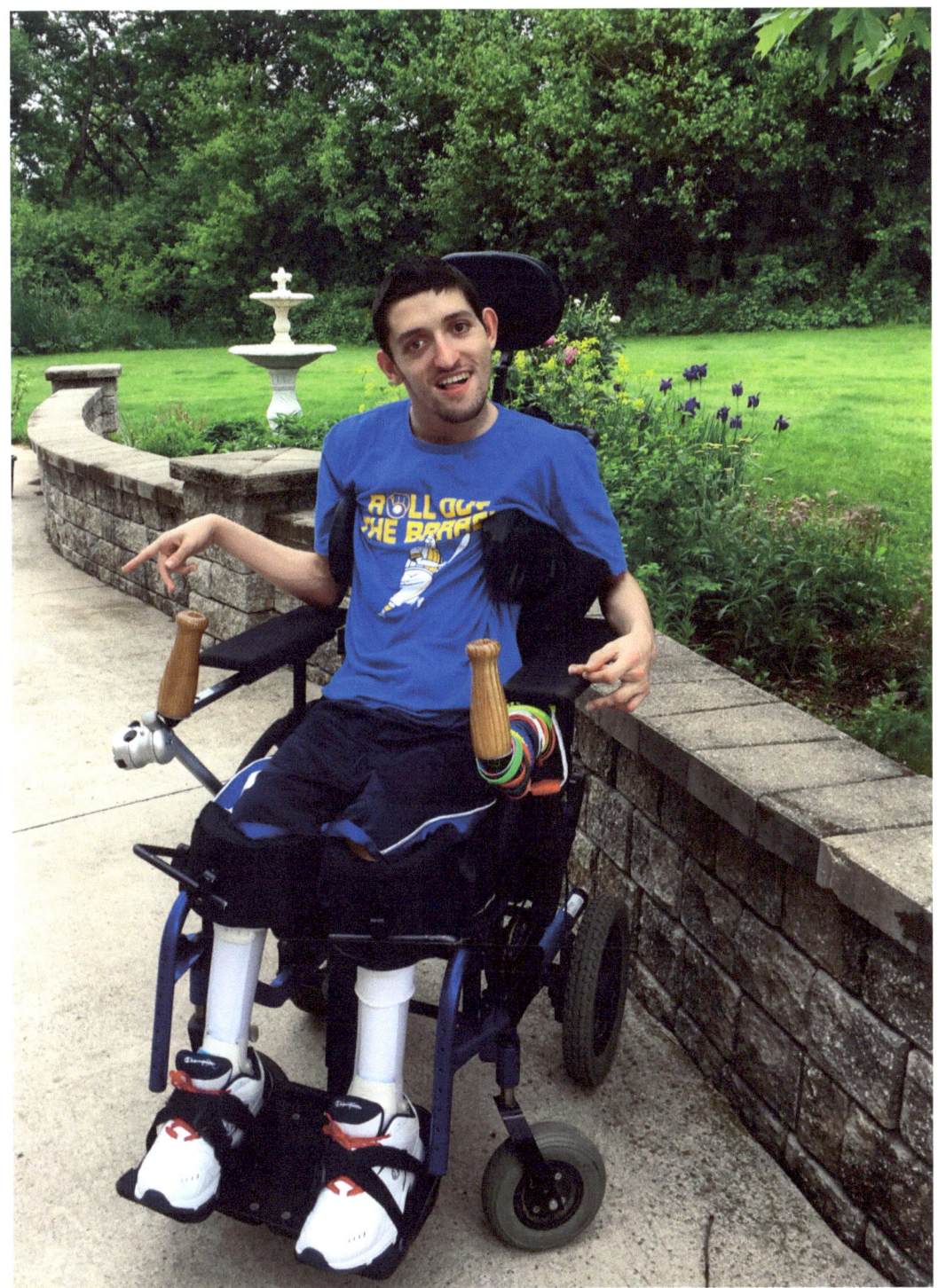

We have a special elevator in our house for Nick.

Every time Rusty hears the elevator door open,

he runs to the elevator and waits for Nick to get in.

Rusty and Nick squeeze into the small elevator together. Rusty is not afraid in the elevator because Nick is always with him as they ride up and down.

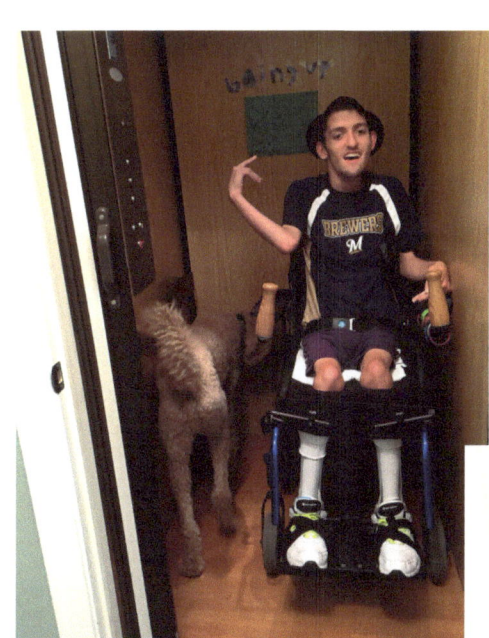
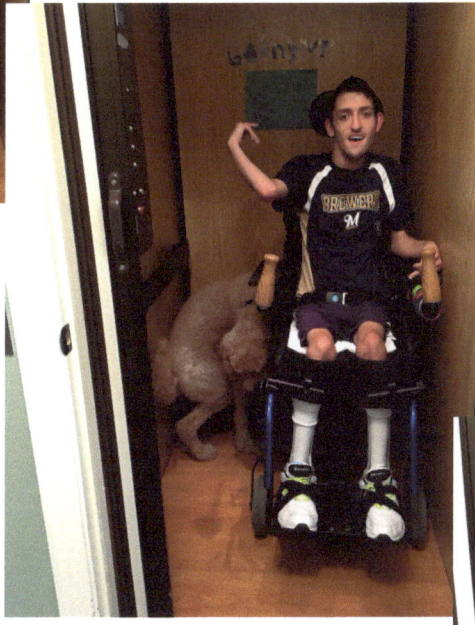

Rusty loves being in the elevator, but most of all, he loves Nick. Whenever Nick's wheelchair stops, Rusty loves to jump onto Nick and give dog kisses.

One day, Rusty got very sick. The vet said there was something wrong with Rusty's stomach and he would need surgery.
Rusty had to stay in the hospital for a few days.

Nick was very sad and worried about Rusty.

After the surgery, the vet gave Rusty a certificate of bravery! He said Rusty would be fine but would need to get lots of rest and could *not* go up and down the stairs.

Nick was so happy to have Rusty home.

He made sure Rusty got plenty of rest. And, Rusty wouldn't need to go up and down the stairs.

After all, Rusty is "The Elevator Dog!"

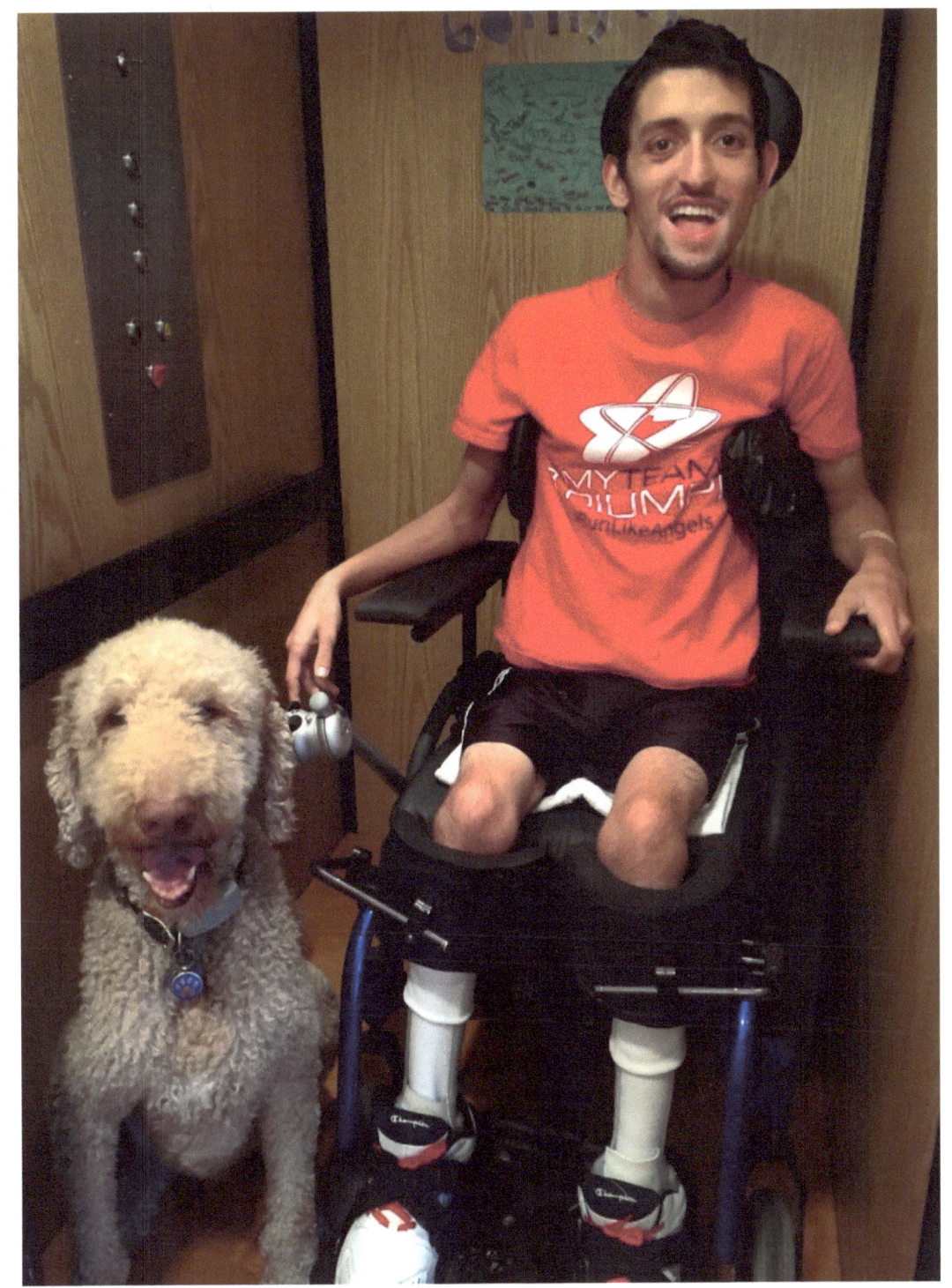

About the Goldendoodle

Rusty and Gigi

A Goldendoodle is a cross between a Golden Retriever and a Poodle. They have the personality traits of both breeds.

Golden Retrievers are very loyal, fun-loving, gentle dogs that like to be around people, are fun to play with, and have good hunting instincts. They like to retrieve balls and other objects, which is one of the reasons why they get their name.

Poodles were originally bred in Germany as a type of hunting dog to retrieve water fowl for the hunter. The German word *Pudelhund*, or "splash-about dog", is where the word 'poodle' comes from. They are easy to train because they are very smart, and are very obedient. Poodles do not shed, so they are a great breed for people like Nick, who are allergic to dogs.

Goldendoodles come in many sizes and colors, including black, white, brown, and apricot. Sometimes, they have a mix of colors...like Rusty, who has a white patch on his chest!

Resource: www.poodlemaineia.com

About Nick

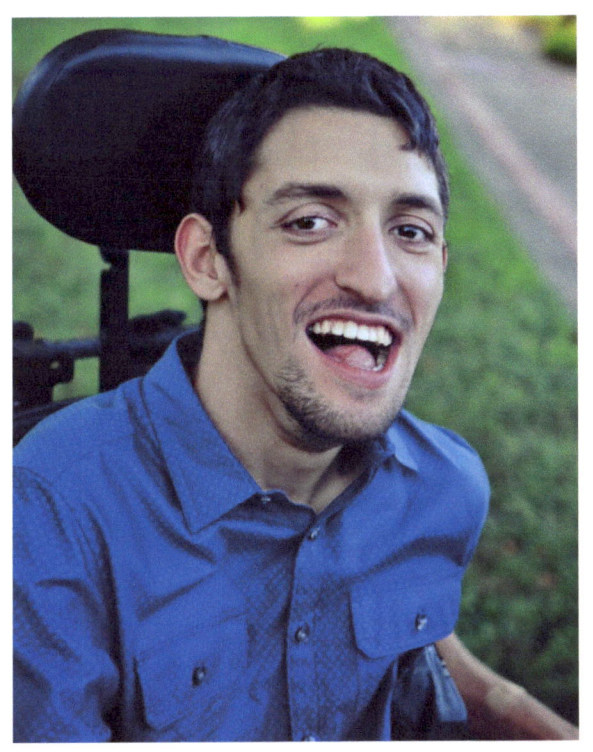

Nick Salerno is the oldest of four children. He was born with Cerebral Palsy, a permanent disability caused by a lack of oxygen he received before he was born. Because of this, he cannot control all of his muscles which means he cannot walk or talk. However, Nick communicates through his eyes and his head movements. He looks to the left to answer 'YES', right to answer 'NO', up to answer 'I DON'T KNOW", and down when he wants you to repeat the question. He makes all of his life choices with his eyes.

Nick is presently a senior in high school and wants to attend college. He loves math, science, and animals, especially his two Goldendoodles, Rusty and Gigi. He also enjoys sports, especially baseball, football, and hockey. His favorite teams are the Milwaukee Brewers, the Green Bay Packers, and the Chicago Blackhawks. Nick plays baseball in a special league for others with disabilities. He also participates in marathons and 5Ks, using a special race chair and assisted by volunteers. Nick is extremely smart and an excellent student. He inspires others to do their very best every day.

Thank You from Rusty

I would like to thank the following people:

My mommy, Nancy, for taking a scared, skinny, shy puppy
and turning him into a handsome prince;

Maria for motivating and encouraging me and Mommy everyday,
and for helping Mommy to write my book;

Victoria for staying up with me during thunderstorms
and making me special blankets;

Alexander for being my play buddy
(even in the house, when we're not supposed to); and

My daddy, Mark, for taking me out when it is
dark and scary at night.

I would also like to thank my special vets
who helped save my life twice:

Dr. Maggie from Regner Veterinary clinic,
Dr. Mary Sue from Westosha Veterinary Hospital
Dr. Baker, the best dog surgeon ever!

But mostly I would like to thank my best friend, *Nicholas*,
for talking to me everyday with his big brown eyes and
letting me ride the elevator of life with him!

When you have a special friend like Nick,
it helps you to be brave!

Who is your special friend in your life?

Love,

The End

www.ingramcontent.com/pod-product-compliance
Lightning Source LLC
Chambersburg PA
CBHW041537040426

42446CB00002B/129